MW01616392

Little
Hawaiian
Liliko'i
Cookbook

by Gail Hercher
photographs by Michael Hercher

MUTUAL PUBLISHING

Library of Congress Control Number: 2012941604

ISBN-10: 1-56647-983-5
ISBN-13: 978-1-56647-983-7

All photos © Michael Hercher unless otherwise credited below:
Dreamstime.com: pg. 12 © Ustel65, pg. 21 © Stanislav Kharlamenkov, pg. 39 © Johnfoto, pg. 43 © Elenamiv

First Printing, September 2012
Second Printing, August 2014

Mutual Publishing, LLC
1215 Center Street, Suite 210
Honolulu, Hawai'i 96816
Ph: 808-732-1709 / Fax: 808-734-4094
E-mail: info@mutualpublishing.com
www.mutualpublishing.com

Printed in South Korea

Table of Contents

Desserts

Liliko'i Basics

Glossary

Introduction

Liliko'i, perhaps Hawai'i's most distinctive fruit, is coveted for its sweet-tart taste, intoxicating fragrance and exquisite color. Hawaiian for "passion fruit," bartenders use liliko'i juice in exotic drinks, bakers add it to wedding and lū'au cakes, cottage industries need it to make jams and jellies, local emporiums rely on it for shave ice, sorbet, sherbet and ice cream, Aunties want it for their special shortbread cookies, and professional chefs use it to "heighten" sauces.

Interestingly, despite the demand for them, fresh liliko'i are hard to find. Supermarkets don't build pyramids of liliko'i in the produce section and they are rarely seen at farmers' markets. Sometimes, it's possible to cadge a few liliko'i from a neighbor; otherwise, the vines can be found in the wild hanging over hiking trails or clinging to trees and fences. Of course, bottled liliko'i juice can be found at food specialty shops or ordered online, but the best way to guarantee an unadulterated supply of fresh juice, is to grow your own. Happily, this is very easy to do; cut a ripe fruit in half, scoop out

the seeds, and plant them immediately in the ground next to a fence or trellis. Because liliko'i grow like a weed (disparagingly called "invasive" by some), one or two seedlings (pollinated by Hawai'i's ever-present carpenter bees), will quickly grow into long vines that will produce nutritious, abundant fruit within a year or two.

The first liliko'i seeds were brought to Hawai'i in 1880 from Australia by Eugene Delmar who planted them on his Maui ranch. The plant spread quickly. Soon, the fruit of *Passiflora Edulis* was a local favorite, referred to by the name of the area in which it was first planted, East Maui's Liliko'i Gulch. Seeds were subsequently taken to the neighbor islands and within a few years the vine was growing wild everywhere—so much so, that it was common for sugar and pineapple plantation workers to pick liliko'i from a fence or tree, squash them open between their knees and suck out the refreshing juice. Before too long, as memories became fuzzy, many people even came to believe that liliko'i was a native plant!

Passiflora, the plant that produces the spectacular flower and edible fruit, was first seen by 16th century Spanish explorers in South America. Later Catholic missionaries, astonished by the intricate structure of this flower and anxious to convert the local population to Catholicism, assigned religious meaning to this exotic flower, asserting that its parts symbolized the Passion of Christ (i.e., Crucifixion). To them, the three stigmas of *Passiflora* represented the Trinity, the five stamens of *Passiflora* represented the hammers used to drive nails into Christ's hands; the mitten-shaped leaves, the pointed hands of the accusers; the ominous, coiling tendrils simulated whips used by the persecutors, and so on.

After the Spanish discovery, explorers, missionaries, and horticulturalists carried *Passiflora* seeds from South America around the world and before long the plant was cultivated in almost every tropical country. Eventually, Eugene Delmar saw the "passion flower" in Australia and took some seeds to Maui where he believed the climate presented favorable growing conditions for the blossom and fruit. Little did he know the effect the plant would have on Hawaiian cooking for it is now a regular ingredient in many drinks and almost a requirement for a lū'au cake.

There are over 500 varieties of *Passiflora* in the world (not all produce edible fruit). It is found in all tropical climates, but California, Central and South America are the primary world producers of this edible fruit and juice.

A few varieties are grown in Hawai'i, but *Passiflora Edulis* (purple fruit) and *Passiflora Edulis Flavicarpa* (yellow fruit) are the most popular for cooking purposes.

Few people remember that during the 1950s there was a fledgling liliko'i industry in Hawai'i with more than 50 liliko'i farmers and eight juice processing plants operating in the state. The University of Hawai'i predicted that liliko'i would become a major source of revenue for the state, but, unfortunately, the unpredictable volume of fruit, the high cost of processing and the long distance to mainland markets caused the industry to lose momentum and fade away. Today, very few farmers grow liliko'i as a crop; instead, it is grown on a small scale in home gardens or as a "casual" crop (i.e. on fences or old trees) by small farmers and sold to local liliko'i enterprises. Much of Hawai'i's liliko'i juice is used to make products for tourists—juice, syrup, curd, jelly, soap, lotions, and candles—as a fragrant reminder of their visit to our beautiful State. Big time liliko'i producers (of canned drinks, and frozen concentrate) import it from other places like California or Ecuador, which ships it in fifty-five gallon drums!

In the years to come, as the State of Hawai'i moves steadily toward sustainability and citizens commit to "eating local," perhaps more farmers and home gardeners will decide to grow liliko'i. If so, they will be rewarded with exquisite flowers and delicious fruit!

DRINKS

Liliko'i Lemon Drop

Serves 2

2-1/2 ounces gin
1 ounce simple syrup
1-1/2 ounces lemon juice
1/2 ounce Cointreau
1/2 ounce lilikoʻi juice

Wet rim of glasses with water and dip into sugar to coat.
Pour ingredients into shaker, add ice and shake until very
cold (30 times). Pour into two martini glasses. Garnish with
mint leaf.

Little Liliko'i Mocktail

Serves 1

This is an easy drink to make for people who don't drink alcohol.

2 ounces liliko'i juice
2 ounces pineapple
1 ounce lemon juice
1 ounce simple syrup
2 ounces diet Coke

Pour ingredients except
for cola into shaker and
shake well. Pour into tall
glass with some ice. Top
with Coke and garnish with
lemon or lime slice and
flower.

Luscious Liliko'i

Serves 2

Here, liliko'i juice is mixed with a special vodka!

2 ounces coconut flavored vodka
2 ounces lemon or lime juice
1 ounce simple syrup
2 ounces liliko'i juice

Wet rim of glasses with water and dip into sugar to coat. Pour ingredients into cocktail shaker. Shake with ice until very cold (30 times). Pour into 2 sugar-rimmed martini glasses. Garnish with slice of lemon or lime.

Hawaiian Mojito with Liliko'i

Serves 2

1-1/2 ounces simple syrup muddled (mashed) with 4 large
   fresh mint leaves
Juice of 1 lime
3 teaspoons liliko'i juice
2 ounces dark rum
4 ounces soda water

Fill cocktail shaker loosely with ice. Add ingredients. Shake
until very cold (30 times). Pour into two tall glasses. Garnish
with mint leaf.

—Inspired by Brad Ricker

Hawaiian Margarita with Liliko'i

Serves 2

This margarita is especially easy to make and drink!

1/3 cup liliko'i juice
1/3 cup Tequila
1/3 cup Cointreau
Dash of agave nectar or sugar syrup

Wet rims of glasses with water and dip into sugar to coat. Fill cocktail shaker with ice. Add juice, alcohol and agave or sugar syrup. Shake with passion. Pour into glasses. Garnish with umbrella and lime slice.

—*Contributed by Canelle Demange*

Local Liliko'i Colada

Serves 2

This drink showcases liliko'i's affinity for coconut!

1/2 cup fresh pineapple, chopped
3 ounces light rum
3 ounces cream of coconut
2 ounces liliko'i juice
4 ounces pineapple juice
2 cups ice

Combine ingredients in blender until smooth. Pour mixture into 2 tall glasses with ice. Garnish with spear of pineapple and mint leaf.

Easy Mai Tai

Serves 2

Liliko'i makes this mai tai special!

2 ounces liliko'i juice
2 ounces lemon juice
2 ounces guava juice
2 ounces orange juice
2 ounces pineapple juice
4 ounces dark rum
1 ounce Cointreau
1 ounce simple syrup

Mix all ingredients in pitcher. Pour over ice into tall glass. Garnish with piece of pineapple, mint leaf and cherry on toothpick.

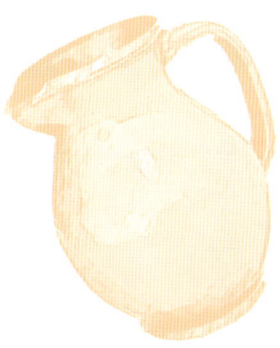

Tequila Passoa

Makes 1 drink

Passoa liqueur may be hard to find, but is worth the search!

1-1/2 ounces Tequila
1 ounce Passoa (passion fruit liqueur)
2 ounces liliko'i juice
1 ounce simple syrup
1 teaspoon lemon juice

Pour Tequila, Passoa, liliko'i juice, sugar syrup and lemon juice into cocktail shaker with ice. Shake vigorously and pour into a martini glass edged with sugar. Garnish with a lemon twist.

Lillet Liliko'i

Serves 1

*Lilikoʻi partnered with this French friend
is unusual and refreshing!*

2 ounces Lillet Blanc (white French apéritif wine)
2 ounces lilikoʻi syrup
2 ounces simple syrup
Soda water

Put ingredients in tall glass. Fill with ice, leaving room for inch of soda water on top. Garnish with mint leaf.

Li Hing Liliko'i

Makes 2 drinks

Chinese li hing mui powder mixed with Liliko'i is so 'ono!

- 1 tablespoon li hing mui powder
- 1 tablespoon sugar
- 2 ounces liliko'i juice
- 1 ounce lemon juice
- 1 ounce lime juice
- 2 ounces Cointreau
- 4 ounces Tequila

Mix li hing mui powder with sugar in wide plate.
Wet rims of margarita glasses with water and dip into li hing mui mixture.

Pour rest of ingredients into shaker and shaker vigorously (30 times). Pour into glasses. Garnish with lime slice.

Pineapple Passion

Makes 2 drinks

Liliko'i and pineapple make a perfect couple!

4 ounces dark rum
4 ounces liliko'i juice
4 ounces pineapple juice
1 ounce simple syrup
1 tablespoon lemon juice
2 dashes Angostura bitters
Soda water

Pour ingredients into shaker. Shake until cold (30 times).
Pour into highball glasses. Top with soda water.
Garnish with wedge of pineapple and cherry.

Rum Punch with Liliko'i

Serves 6 to 8

Everyone loves a red-colored punch during the holidays!

4 ounces liliko'i juice
4 ounces acai juice
4 ounces cranberry juice
2 ounces orange juice
2 ounces lemon juice
2 cups pineapple juice
1 large bottle ginger ale
8 ounces dark rum

Mix all ingredients in pitcher. Pour over ice into tall hurricane glasses. Garnish with a piece of pineapple, mint leaf and cherry on toothpick.

Virgin Liliko'i Punch

Serves 8 to 12

This punch is popular with teens and grownups alike!

1 cup liliko'i juice
2 cups pineapple juice
2 cups guava juice
2 cups cranberry juice
8 cups tea, chilled (Brew ahead using 4 tea bags. Liliko'i tea is
   highly recommended, but other teas can be substituted.)
2 (28 ounce) bottles ginger ale, chilled
Ice block
1 orange, sliced thinly
1 star fruit, sliced thinly

On the day before party, make an ice block in a container to fit punchbowl. Combine all ingredients except ginger ale in large pitcher or bowl. Just before serving, pour over ice block in punch bowl. Add ginger ale and garnish with slices of orange and star fruit.

Liliko'i Sangria

Serves 8

1 cup liliko'i juice
1 cup orange juice
1 cup pineapple juice
1/4 cup Cointreau
1 bottle white wine
1/2 cup brandy
1/2 cup simple syrup
1 orange, thinly sliced and halved
Handful of fresh mint leaves

Combine liliko'i juice, orange juice, Cointreau, wine, brandy and simple syrup in large pitcher. Refrigerate until cold. Pour into glasses over ice. Garnish with orange slice and mint.

Island Liliko'i Smoothie

Serves 2

Protein powder makes this drink extra healthy!

2 bananas
1 mango or papaya
1 cup cow, almond or coconut milk
1/2 cup liliko'i juice
1/2 cup orange juice
4 scoops vanilla protein powder

Combine bananas, fruit and milk in food processor. Blend until smooth. Add juices and powder (1 cup of any juice will work). Blend well. Garnish with mint leaves.

Liliko'i Sports Cooler

Serves 1

Keep this nearby in a thermos for any sports activity!

1/4 cup liliko'i juice
1 cup orange juice
Juice of one lemon
Soda water

Pour liliko'i juice, orange juice and lemon juice over ice into tall glass. Top with soda water.

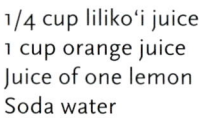

SIDES &
SAUCES

Baked Beans with Liliko'i Syrup

Serves 6

These beans have extra tang!

1 (28 ounce) can honey baked beans, drained
1 (15 ounce) can black beans, drained
1/4 cup brown sugar
4 strips bacon, cooked until very crisp
1 medium onion, sliced thin
1 clove garlic
3 dashes hot sauce
1/2 cup liliko'i syrup

Preheat oven to 350°F. Fry bacon until very crisp, saving drippings in pan. Crumble and set aside. Fry onion rings and garlic in bacon drippings until very limp. Drain on paper towel. Mix beans, sugar and onion mixture together in casserole with lid. Bake for 30 minutes. Remove from oven. Stir in liliko'i juice and top with bacon bits.

Spicy Liliko‘i ‘Ahi Poke

Serves 2 as appetizer

Heaven is two local favorites combined!

1 pound ‘ahi, cut into 3/4-inch cubes
1 clove garlic, chopped fine
2 tablespoons onion, chopped
1 green onion, cut fine with scissors
1 avocado, cut into 3/4-inch chunks
1/4 cup limu
1 teaspoon shoyu
3 tablespoons mayonnaise
2 tablespoons liliko‘i juice
1/2 teaspoon Sriracha, or to taste

———————————————————————

Combine ‘ahi, garlic, onions, avocado, limu and shoyu.

Mix together mayonnaise, liliko‘i juice and Sriracha.

Add to ‘ahi mixture. Chill before serving.

Love's Liliko'i Cole Slaw

Serves 4 to 6

This cole slaw is very popular on the Big Island!

1 medium head green cabbage, shredded
2 medium carrots, shredded
2 Granny Smith apples, diced small
1/2 small pineapple, crushed and drained
1 cup raisins
1/2 cup macadamia nuts, chopped
1/2 cup unsweetened shredded coconut

1 cup mayonnaise
1/4 cup liliko'i syrup

Mix ingredients from cabbage to coconut in large bowl.

Mix mayonnaise and liliko'i syrup in small bowl. Pour into large bowl. Toss ingredients. Chill several hours to blend flavors.

—*Contributed by Margy Love, Love Family Farm,*
Captain Cook, HI

Deviled Liliko'i Eggs

Serves 6

Liliko'i juice and sweet chili sauce make these eggs special!

12 hardboiled eggs
1 tablespoon sour cream
1 tablespoon mayonnaise
1 tablespoon smooth Dijon mustard
1 tablespoon liliko'i juice
Salt and pepper to taste

Garnish:
12 tiny sprigs parsley
12 capers
1/4 cup sweet chili sauce

Cut eggs in half. Scoop out yolks, mash in bowl with sour cream, mustard, liliko'i juice, salt and pepper. Return yolk mixture to egg halves with spoon or cookie gun. Garnish each with one sprig of parsley and one caper. Serve with chili sauce.

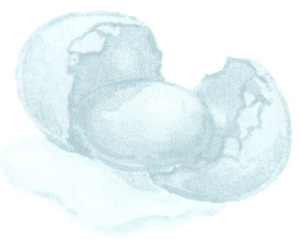

Namasu with Liliko'i Juice
(Sweet Japanese Cucumber)

4 small servings

A good, quick, sweet, crunchy, no-fat pickle!

1 cucumber, sliced very thin
3 tablespoons carrot, sliced very thin
3 tablespoons sugar
3 tablespoons white vinegar
1 tablespoon liliko'i juice
1/8 teaspoon black sesame seeds

Combine cucumber, carrot, sugar, vinegar, and liliko'i juice. Chill until very cold. Serve on small decorative plate. Sprinkle with a few black sesame seeds.

Liliko'i Dipping Sauce

Serves 2

This unusual sauce is excellent with pot stickers!

1/2 inch piece ginger root, grated
1 clove garlic, chopped fine
1 pinch red pepper flakes
2 green onions, chopped fine
1 tablespoon mirin
3 tablespoons white vinegar
1/4 cup liliko'i juice
1 teaspoon sesame oil
1 tablespoon cornstarch
1 tablespoon water

Mix cornstarch into cold water until smooth. Heat until slightly thickened. Add other ingredients. Serve warm in small bowls with potstickers or steamed vegetables.

—*Originally appeared in* Our Hānai Plate

Sam Choy's Mango-Liliko'i-Basil Shrimp

Serves 4

A very tasty and beautiful shrimp dish!

1 pound shrimp, shells on (16/20 count)
2 large mangoes, each cut in 6 large chunks

Marinade:
1/2 cup mango puree
1/2 cup liliko'i juice
1 tablespoon brown sugar
1 tablespoon fresh basil, minced
1 tablespoon fresh dill, chopped
1 teaspoon fresh ginger, minced
1/2 teaspoon garlic, minced

Peel and de-vein shrimp, leaving tails on. Combine marinade ingredients and marinate shrimp for 1 hour.

On each of four skewers, alternately thread shrimp and mango chunks.

Grill or broil kabobs for 7 minutes, or until shrimp is cooked, turning once and basting occasionally with marinade.

—*Originally appeared in* Aloha Cuisine

Vegetable Liliko'i Salsa

Serves 4 with shrimp as appetizer

You can substitute other vegetables, but keep the liliko'i!

1/2 cup cucumber, chopped into 1/2-inch pieces
1/2 cup green pepper, chopped into 1/2-inch pieces
1/2 cup red pepper, chopped into 1/2-inch pieces
1/2 cup pineapple, chopped into 1/2-inch pieces
1/2 cup mango, chopped into 1/2-inch pieces
1/4 cup onion, chopped fine
1/2 teaspoon hot pepper, chopped very fine (optional)
1 garlic clove, chopped fine
1/2 cup lemon juice
1/2 cup liliko'i juice
Salt and pepper to taste
1 pound medium shrimp, cooked, chopped, and cold

Combine all ingredients EXCEPT shrimp. Refrigerate for several hours. Add shrimp just before serving.

Mango Fig Liliko'i Chutney

Makes 4 cups

A surprisingly good accompaniment with curry & rice!

1/2 pound dried figs
1/2 cup Cointreau
1/2 cup raisins
2 mangoes, sliced
1 onion, sliced
2 cloves garlic
1/2 teaspoon red pepper flakes
1/2 teaspoon Sriracha
1 cup sugar
1/2 cup vinegar
1/8 teaspoon nutmeg
1/8 teaspoon cloves
8 tablespoons liliko'i juice

Soak figs and raisins in Cointreau overnight. Peel and slice mangoes. Cook in microwave on high for 5 minutes. Mix everything together EXCEPT Liliko'i juice in saucepan.

Simmer until very thick, stirring frequently. Divide into 4 freezer bags. Add 2 tablespoons of liliko'i juice to each bag. Freeze until ready to serve.

Mustard Liliko'i Sauce

Serves 4

This simple sauce is wonderful on meat or fish!

2 tablespoons mayonnaise
2 tablespoons sour cream
2 tablespoons coarse ground Dijon mustard
2 tablespoons liliko'i juice

Mix all ingredients together.

Serve with cold meat or salmon.

Coconut Curry Liliko'i Sauce

Makes 2 cups

Keep a supply of this sauce on hand; it's good on everything!

1 tablespoon olive oil
1 tablespoon sesame oil
3 tablespoons onion, chopped fine
2 cloves garlic, chopped fine
1 to 2 tablespoons curry powder
1/2 teaspoon Sriracha (or more)
1 tablespoon shoyu
1 tablespoon sugar
1 (13.5 ounce) can coconut milk
1 stalk lemongrass, cut into 3-inch pieces
Salt to taste
1/2 cup fresh basil leaves, cut with scissors
1 teaspoon cornstarch
2 tablespoons liliko'i juice

Heat oils. Saute onion, garlic, and curry powder until onion is soft and mixture is fragrant. Add shoyu, sugar, salt, coconut milk and lemongrass. Simmer 15 minutes.

Remove lemongrass pieces. Mix cornstarch with 2 tablespoons water. Add to coconut mixture. Cook until thickened. Just before serving, add liliko'i juice and cut basil leaves. Pour over rice, chicken or vegetables.

Mango Liliko‘i Soup

Serves 4 to 6

This exotic soup will surprise and delight everyone!

2 cups liliko‘i juice
2 tablespoons orange juice
2 tablespoons cornstarch
4 tablespoons water
4 egg yolks
1 cup white wine
3 mangoes
2 tablespoons sugar
1/2 cup heavy cream
2 tablespoons Cointreau

Garnish:
2 avocado, diced into
   1/2-inch squares
2 tablespoons fresh chives, chopped fine

Puree juices with mangoes in food processor. Dissolve cornstarch in water. Add to juice mixture. Pour into top of double boiler. Mix egg yolks with white wine. Pour into juice mixture. Over medium heat, whisk continuously, until thickened. Remove from heat. When cool, add heavy cream and Cointreau. Garnish with avocado and chives.

Barbeque Sauce with Liliko'i

For 2 pounds of meat or fish

Liliko'i will add a subtle tart-sweet taste to your meat!

1 tablespoon oil
1/4 cup onion, chopped fine
2 garlic cloves
1/2 teaspoon red pepper, chopped
1 quarter-sized piece of ginger, chopped
1 cup ketchup
1/2 cup liliko'i juice
1 teaspoon Worcestershire sauce
1 teaspoon horseradish
1/4 cup brown sugar
1/2 teaspoon cumin powder
1/2 teaspoon celery seed
Salt and pepper to taste

Cook first five ingredients in small saucepan until soft. Add remaining ingredients. Simmer until reduced to 1 cup.

Sweet Liliko'i Salad Dressing

Serves 4

A fresh salad with this dressing makes a great lunch!

1/2 cup macadamia nut or olive oil
1/4 cup liliko'i juice
1 tablespoon onion, chopped
1 clove garlic
1 cup mayonnaise
1 teaspoon lemon juice
1 teaspoon sugar
1 teaspoon coarse Dijon
   mustard
2 tablespoons salsa verde
2 tablespoons parsley
2 tablespoons cilantro
2 tablespoons dill
Salt and pepper to taste

Pulse all ingredients together in small food processor until fully blended.

DESSERTS

Pudding Cakes with Liliko‘i Bottom

Serves 6

These little cakes have a surprise at the bottom—pudding!

1 cup sugar
1/4 cup flour
1/8 teaspoon baking powder
4 large eggs, separated
2 tablespoons unsalted butter, softened
3/4 cup whole milk
1/2 cup liliko'i juice
1/2 teaspoon salt

Heat oven to 350°F. Place 6 ramekins inside roasting pan.

In medium bowl, mix together sugar and flour; set aside. In another bowl, mix eggs yolks and butter until smooth. Stir in milk and liliko'i juice. Add juice mixture to sugar mixture. Stir until smooth.

Beat egg white and salt until stiff peaks form. Slowly fold egg whites into liliko'i mixture.

Divide pudding mixture among the six ramekins. Fill each ramekin about 2/3 full. Add water to roasting pan to reach halfway up sides of ramekins. Bake until tops are golden, 30 to 40 minutes.

Liliko'i Chiffon Squares

Serves 12

These squares are particularly popular at birthday parties!

Crust:
2 cups flour
1/4 cup sugar
1 cup butter, chilled (2 blocks)
3/4 cup chopped nuts, optional

Mix ingredients, except nuts, with pastry blender until it is a sandy texture. Add nuts if desired. Press into 9 x 13 inch pan.

Bake at 350°F for 15 minutes. Chill well.

Filling:
1 pint carton whipping cream, whipped
1 (8 ounce) package cream cheese
1/2 cup sugar
1/2 teaspoon vanilla

Mix cream cheese and sugar until smooth and soft. Add vanilla and whipped cream. Spread over crust. Refrigerate until firm.

Topping:
1 envelope unflavored gelatin (1 tablespoon)
1/4 cup cold water
4 eggs, separated
1/2 cup sugar
1/4 teaspoon salt
3/4 cup liliko'i juice
3 tablespoons lemon juice
1/4 cup sugar
1 (8 ounce) container Cool Whip

Soften gelatin in cold water. Set aside. Stirring constantly, cook egg yolks, 1/2 cup sugar, salt and liliko'i juice on medium heat until thickened. Add lemon juice. Stir in softened gelatin. Remove from heat and cool completely.

Beat egg whites on high speed. Slowly add 1/2 cup sugar and continue beating until stiff peaks form. Fold in liliko'i mixture. Spread over filling and refrigerate until set. Top with Cool Whip.

—Originally appeared in Hawai'i's Best Local Desserts

Raspberry Liliko'i Freezer Cake

Serves 6

Make this cool cake in the morning for a hot night!

2 packages ladyfingers
1/4 cup cold water
1 envelope (1 tablespoon) unflavored gelatin
1 cup liliko'i juice
1/4 cup Cointreau
1/2 cup + 2 tablespoons sugar
1 cup heavy cream
1/2 teaspoon vanilla
1 small bag frozen raspberries, thawed
2 teaspoons confectioners' sugar, or more to taste
1 teaspoon lemon juice
1 cup fresh raspberries for garnish

Line loaf pan with plastic wrap to overhang top edge on all sides. Line sides of pan with ladyfingers, rounded ends facing bottom and rounded sides facing out.

Sprinkle gelatin over cold water to soften in medium bowl. Combine liliko'i juice and 1/2 cup sugar in small saucepan. Cook over medium heat, stirring, until sugar dissolves. Stir in gelatin mixture and cook until slightly thickened.

In large bowl, whip heavy cream with 2 tablespoons of sugar and 1/2 teaspoon vanilla until it holds soft peaks. Fold liliko'i mixture into whipped cream. Pour 1/2 liliko'i mixture into center of prepared loaf pan. Submerge two layers of ladyfingers into mousse, pressing down. Cover with remaining liliko'i mousse. Freeze at least 6 hours.

Mix defrosted raspberries in blender until smooth. Strain through seive to remove seeds. Stir in confectioners' sugar and lemon juice.

To loosen cake from pan, place bottom in hot water for one minute. Unmold cake by gently tugging at overhanging plastic wrap to loosen. Pull cake out. Peel away plastic wrap. Place cake on plate and put in freezer until serving time.

Thaw for 1 hour before serving. Slice cake. Garnish each slice with drizzled raspberry sauce and fresh raspberries.

Liliko'i Cream Pie

Serves 8

This traditional cream pie is always welcome!

9 graham crackers
6 tablespoons unsalted butter, melted
2 tablespoons sugar
2 large eggs
1 (14 ounce) can sweetened, condensed milk
1/2 cup liliko'i juice
1 teaspoon lemon juice
1/4 teaspoon salt

Heat oven to 350°F. In food processor, grind graham crackers into fine crumbs. Mix crumbs with butter and sugar. Press firmly onto bottom and sides of 9-inch pie plate. Bake 10 minutes. Cool.

In medium bowl, mix eggs, condensed milk, liliko'i juice, lemon juice and salt. Pour mixture into crust and bake 20 minutes, or until firm in center. Refrigerate several hours. To serve, garnish with chopped fresh strawberries and dollop of whipped cream.

Liliko'i Snowballs

Makes about 3 dozen cookies

These cookies are as close as you'll get to snow in Honolulu!

8 ounces unsalted butter, room temperature
2/3 cup confectioners' sugar
3 teaspoons liliko'i juice
Pinch salt
1/4 cup macadamia nuts, chopped finely
1/4 cup sweetened coconut, shredded
3 cups flour
1 cup confectioners' sugar (for rolling)

Heat oven to 325°F. Mix butter and sugar together until creamy. Add liliko'i juice and salt. Mix until combined. Add nuts, coconut and flour. Shape dough into 1-inch balls. Set them on parchment-lined baking sheets. Bake until cookies are light golden brown, 15 to 20 minutes. Allow cookies to cook slightly, but while still warm, roll them in sugar.

Coconut Liliko'i Tapioca Pudding

Serves 6

This red, white and blue dessert is perfect for July 4th!

1/4 cup Minute tapioca
1/3 cup sugar
1 egg
1 cup milk
1 can coconut milk
1 teaspoon vanilla
1/2 cup liliko'i
   juice
1/4 cup raspberry
   jam, thinned
   with 1 teaspoon
   water
3 teaspoons vanilla
   yogurt
6 large blueberries

Mix tapioca, sugar, egg, milk, coconut milk and vanilla in saucepan. Let sit 5 minutes. Cook until boiling, reduce heat, stir constantly until thick. Remove from heat. Cool to room temperature, then add liliko'i juice. Pour into 6 small bowls, ramekins or glasses. Invert onto small plates (optional). Garnish with thinned raspberry jam, dot of yogurt and one blueberry.

Banana Bread with Liliko'i Curd

Makes one loaf

*Enjoy this dark banana bread with liliko'i curd
and fresh Kona coffee!*

3 or 4 ripe bananas
1/3 cup melted butter
1 cup sugar
1 egg, beaten
1 teaspoon vanilla
1 teaspoon baking soda
Pinch of salt
1-1/2 cups flour
1/2 cup macadamia
   nuts, chopped
1/2 cup liliko'i syrup (see
   recipe on page 92)
1/2 cup liliko'i curd (see
   recipe on page 93)

Preheat oven to 350°F. Mix butter into bananas in large bowl.
Mix in sugar, egg and vanilla. Sprinkle baking soda and
salt over mixture. Add flour. Mix only until ingredients are
blended. Pour into buttered 4 x 8 inch loaf pan. Bake 1 hour.
While still warm, make 8 equally spaced holes with wooden
skewer, one inch deep, into top of loaf. Gently pour liliko'i
syrup into holes. Let sit for one hour before slicing. Serve
with liliko'i curd.

Liliko'i Mochi

Makes 24 pieces

A modern approach to making traditional Japanese candy!

2-1/2 cups mochiko (rice flour)
2 cups sugar
2 cups liliko'i juice
1 cup water
2 to 3 tablespoons lemon or lime juice
1/2 cup kinako (soy bean powder)
   OR katakuriko (potato starch)

Combine all ingredients and pour into a greased tube pan or microwaveable bundt pan. Cover with plastic wrap. Microwave on high for 10 to 12 minutes. Remove plastic wrap immediately and cool. Remove to a cutting board dusted with kinako or potato katakuriko. Cut into pieces and coat each piece with kinako or katakuriko.

—*Contributed by Alberta Lau*

Lūʻau Lilikoʻi Cake

Serves 12 to 16

Eat this delicious cake with fork or fingers at your next lūʻau!

Cake:
1 cup butter
1-1/2 cups sugar
4 eggs
1/2 cup milk
1 tablespoon vanilla extract
2-1/4 cups flour
2 teaspoons baking powder
1/2 teaspoon salt

Preheat oven to 350°F. Butter and flour 9 x 13-inch pan. Mix butter and sugar until smooth and creamy in large bowl. Add eggs, milk and vanilla. Combine flour, sugar, baking powder and salt in large bowl; add gradually to egg mixture. Scrape thick batter from bowl into pan. Bake 30 minutes or until toothpick comes out clean. Cool on rack. REFRIGERATE.

Lilikoʻi Butter Frosting:
8 ounce package cream cheese, softened
1/4 cup unsalted butter, softened
1 cup confectioners' sugar
1 teaspoon lilikoʻi juice
1/2 teaspoon lemon zest

Combine cheese with butter until smooth and creamy. Mix in liliko'i juice and zest. Using rubber spatula, cover cake with frosting. Pipe or otherwise create a border of frosting around top perimeter of cake. Refrigerate to set frosting.

Liliko'i Gel Topping :
(make this while frosted cake is chilling)
2 tablespoons cornstarch mixed with 1/2 cup cold water
1-1/2 cups liliko'i juice
1 teaspoon lemon juice
2 egg yolks
Pinch of salt
1 tablespoon butter

Garnish:
Shredded coconut
Lilikoi seeds

Stir cornstarch and water in double boiler until smooth. Stir in liliko'i juice, lemon juice, egg yolks and salt. Cook until definitely thickened, stirring constantly. Remove from heat. Stir in butter. Cool somewhat. Spread cool gel on top of frosted, refrigerated cake, inside border of frosting or coconut. Refrigerate until firm. Sprinkle with shredded coconut and a few liliko'i seeds.

Heavenly Liliko‘i Bars

Makes 32 small bars

You'll be a star when you bring out these bars!

1 cup butter, room temperature
1 cup sugar
2 cups flour
1/2 teaspoon baking powder
1-1/2 cups liliko'i curd (make this first; see recipe on page 93)
2/3 cup flaked coconut
1/2 cup macadamia nuts, chopped

Preheat oven to 375°F. Line a 9 x 13 x 3 inch baking pan with foil, allowing it to hang over edges. Grease foil; set aside.

Beat butter with sugar until creamy. Add flour and baking powder. Mix with spoon until just combined. Reserve 2/3 cup of the crumb mixture; set aside. Press remaining crumb mixture with fingers onto bottom of prepared pan. Bake for 8 minutes.

Remove pan from oven. Spread curd over crust in pan. Combine remaining crumbs, coconut and chopped nuts and sprinkle over liliko'i curd. Bake 20 minutes or until lightly browned. Use edges of foil to lift uncut bars out of pan. Cut into square or triangular bars.

Coconut Liliko'i Cheesecake

Serves 12

Is this the best cheesecake ever?

Crust:

1 cup sweetened, shredded coconut
1 cup graham crackers, finely ground
1/2 cup flour
1/2 cup macadamia nuts, chopped
1/2 cup sugar
1/2 cup unsalted butter, cut into pieces

Preheat oven to 350°F. Blend coconut, graham cracker crumbs, sugar, nuts and flour onto bottom of 9-inch spring-form pan, pushing up sides. Bake until golden, about 15 minutes. Cool.

Filling:
4 packages (2 pounds) cream cheese
2/3 cup sugar
1 (15 ounce) can cream of coconut milk
1/2 cup liliko'i juice
1/4 teaspoon vanilla extract
1/8 teaspoon salt
4 large eggs plus 2 yolks

Preheat oven to 425°F. Blend cheese, sugar, coconut milk, vanilla, salt and liliko'i juice in food processor. Add eggs. Pour filling into crust. Bake 10 minutes. Reduce oven temperature to 250°F. Bake another 1-1/2 hours. Turn off oven, keep door closed. Let cake cool in oven for one hour, then refrigerate.

Curd *(makes 2 cups)*:
1 cup sugar
1/3 cup butter
1 tablespoon lemon zest
1 tablespoon water
1 teaspoon cornstarch
3 eggs plus 1 egg yolk
1/2 cup liliko'i juice

Combine sugar, butter, lemon zest, eggs and juice in saucepan. Mix cornstarch into water and add to saucepan. Cook over medium heat, *stirring constantly* (about 10 minutes), until as thick as mayonnaise. Pour into glass jar or container. Cool.

Cover cooled cake with curd topping (save some to have with toast!) and dot with liliko'i seeds. Refrigerate cake at least 12 hours before serving.

Almond Pound Cake with Liliko'i Frosting

Makes 1 loaf

Not your grandmother's pound cake!

1-1/2 cups flour
2-1/2 teaspoons baking powder
1/2 teaspoon salt
1/2 cup almonds, chopped fine
3/4 cup butter, softened
1-1/2 cups sugar
1-1/2 cups ricotta cheese
3 eggs
1 teaspoon almond extract
1 (8 ounce) package cream cheese
1/4 cup butter, softened
1 cup confectioners' sugar
2 tablespoons liliko'i juice
1/2 teaspoon grated lemon zest
2 drops yellow food coloring

Cake:

Preheat oven to 350°F. Grease loaf pan. In medium bowl, combine flour, nuts, baking powder, and salt. In larger bowl, mix butter and sugar until creamy. Add cottage cheese, eggs and extract. With wooden spoon, gradually add flour mixture.

Pour batter into loaf pan. Bake at 350°F for 30 minutes.
Reduce heat to 325°F and bake another 30 minutes or until
toothpick inserted in center comes out clean. Remove cake
from oven. Cool in pan for 10 minutes. Invert onto plate.
Spread frosting on top and sides of cake when cool.

Frosting:
Combine cream cheese, sugar, butter, juice and zest until
very smooth. Spread onto cake with small rubber spatula.
Refrigerate until ready to serve.

Passiflora Cake

Serves 12

An edible flower from your kitchen—perfect with tea!

1/4 cup shortbread cookies, ground fine
2-1/2 cups flour
2 teaspoons baking powder
1/2 teaspoon salt
1 cup unsalted butter, softened
2 cups sugar
4 eggs
1 cup milk
Zest of 2 lemons
1 teaspoon lemon juice

Cake:

Preheat oven to 350°F. Butter bundt pan, dust with shortbread crumbs. Sift flour, salt and baking powder. Set aside.

In large bowl, cream butter and sugar until smooth. With spoon, mix in milk, zest and lemon juice until combined. Turn batter into bundt pan. Bake for 1 hour 10 minutes or until cake tester comes out dry. Let cake stand for 3 minutes. Cover with rack, invert cake, remove from pan.

Liliko'i Glaze:
(make glaze after cake is baked as it must be applied immediately)
1/2 cup liliko'i juice
3/4 cups confectioners' sugar

Mix juice and sugar together until absolutely smooth. Drizzle slowly over top of warm cake in flower pattern (to imitate passion flower). Let cake cool completely in refrigerator. Do not cut for several hours. Garnish with flower in center of cake.

—Inspired by Calissa Ricker

Liliko'i Mousse

Serves 4

This North Shore artist's dessert is smooth and beautiful!

1 teaspoon gelatin + 2 tablespoons cold water
2/3 cup liliko'i juice
2 egg yolks, beaten
6 tablespoons sugar
3 drops yellow food coloring
Pinch salt
2/3 cup heavy cream

Garnish:
1 cup fresh raspberries
3 teaspoons raspberry jam thinned with 1 teaspoon water

In small dish, stir 1 teaspoon gelatin with 2 tablespoons cold water until softened. In top of double boiler, mix 2/3 cups liliko'i juice, egg yolks, sugar and salt. Cook until slightly thickened. Stir in gelatin. Cool. In another bowl, whip heavy cream until it holds soft peaks. Whisk liliko'i mixture until fluffy. Fold in the whipped cream. Scoop into glasses and chill well, 3 to 5 hours. Garnish with fresh raspberries and thinned jam.

—Contributed by Judy Nelson, Mokulēia

Mango Liliko‘i Shortcakes

Serves 4

Liliko‘i and mango rejuvenate this traditional recipe!

1 package ladyfingers
1 cup heavy cream
1/2 teaspoon vanilla extract
1 teaspoon sugar
4 mangoes (about 2-1/2 cups), cut into 3/4-inch chunks
1/2 cup liliko‘i juice

Whip cream with vanilla and sugar until it forms soft peaks. Puree 1/2 cup mango chunks with liliko‘i juice. For each serving, place 3 ladyfinger halves on plate. Lather with whipped cream. Spoon 1/4 cup mango chunks on top of cream. Place 3 ladyfinger halves on top. Lather again with whipped cream. Drizzle puree onto cream and top with remaining mango chunks. Garnish with a few liliko‘i seeds.

Liliko'i Crème Brûlée

Serves 4

Liliko'i adds a whole new dimension to crème brûlée!

1 cup heavy cream
1 cup milk
1/2 cup sugar
4 cups egg yolks
1 teaspoon vanilla
1/4 cup liliko'i juice
2 tablespoons white sugar
2 tablespoons brown sugar

Preheat oven to 350°F. Bring half of milk and cream to boil. Add rest of milk, cream and egg yolks. Add vanilla and liliko'i juice, stirring. Pour into 4 ramekins. Bake in water bath 35 to 40 minutes. Chill in refrigerator. When ready to serve, mix white and brown sugars. Sprinkle onto ramekins. Use tiny torch to melt and brown sugar tops.

—Originally appeared in What Maui Likes to Eat

Fruit Tart
with Liliko'i Custard

Serves 8

Liliko'i makes a traditional custard tart seem new!

Crust:
1-1/2 cups shredded, sweetened coconut
9 graham crackers
1 cup flour
1/2 cup ground macadamia nuts
1/2 cup sugar
1/2 cup butter, softened

Custard:
2 egg yolks
1/4 cup sugar
1/4 cup flour
1 cup milk
2 teaspoons vanilla
1/4 cup liliko'i juice
Assortment of fresh fruit to decorate top of tart
1/2 cup liliko'i jelly, thinned with 1/2 teaspoon hot water

Preheat oven to 350°F. With fingers, mix coconut, graham crumbs, flour, nuts, sugar and butter in springform pan. Bake for 20 minutes.

Meanwhile, whisk yolks, sugar, flour and vanilla until thickened. Pour into top of double boiler on top of simmering water. Microwave milk for 30 seconds. Drizzle milk slowly into egg mixture, stirring continuously. Cook 5 to 10 minutes until very thick (like mayonnaise). Remove from heat. Slowly add liliko'i juice and mix well. Spoon custard onto baked crust. Refrigerate for one hour. Decorate with fresh fruit and brush with thinned jelly to seal and make shiny.

Shortbread Cookies with Liliko'i Glaze

Makes 3 dozen small cookies

Use a pineapple cookie cutter to make these Island cookies!

Cookies:
1 cup butter, softened
1 cup confectioners' sugar
2 teaspoons liliko'i juice
1 egg
2 cups flour
1/2 cup ground macadamia nuts
1/2 cup confectioners' sugar
2 teaspoons liliko'i juice

Icing:
1/2 cup confectioners' sugar
2 teaspoons liliko'i juice

Chocolate tips:
1/4 cup bittersweet chocolate chips

Combine butter and sugar until creamy. Add 2 teaspoons liliko'i juice and 1 egg. Mix well. Slowly add flour and nuts. Do not overstir. With floured hands, divide sticky dough into 3 parts. Make each part into a pancake and pat between 2 sheets of plastic wrap to be 1/2-inch thick. Refrigerate until firm, about one hour.

Preheat oven to 350°F. Line cookie pans with paper.

Working with one pancake at a time, pat dough with floured hands until dough is slightly less than 1/2-inch thick. Cut with small cookie cutter. Place on cookie pan. Bake for 10 to 15 minutes, until edges turn brown. Cool.

Mix sugar and lilikoʻi juice together. Brush onto a part of each cookie. Garnish with lilikoʻi seeds (optional).

Heat chocolate chips with 3 tablespoons water for one minute in microwave. Brush melted chocolate on remaining part of cookie.

Liliko'i Sherbet

Serves 6

This sherbet served with shortbread cookies is truly memorable!

1 cup evaporated milk
1 cup coconut milk
1 cup liliko'i juice
1 cup sugar
1/2 teaspoon lemon juice

Whip evaporated milk until light. Whip in coconut milk. Add liliko'i juice, sugar and lemon juice. Freeze for 2 hours. Stir. Freeze another hour. Stir again and pour into food processor. Beat until smooth and opaque. Freeze in plastic container that is tall enough to accommodate an ice cream scoop.

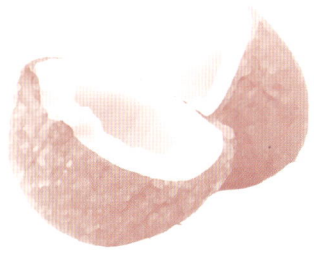

Liliko'i Sorbet

Serves 6

A very refreshing mixture at the end of a long, hot day!

1-3/4 cups sugar
1/2 cup liliko'i juice
1-1/2 cups water
1 teaspoon lemon juice
1 teaspoon lemon zest
1 egg white

Stir sugar into liliko'i juice and water until dissolved. Add lemon juice and zest. Freeze in shallow container. When mixture is frozen (about 2 hours) break up slightly and put in food processor with egg white. Beat until smooth. Freeze in plastic container that is tall enough to accommodate an ice cream scoop.

LILIKOʻI
BASICS

Making Juice, Syrup, Curd & Jelly

All liliko'i cooking begins with liliko'i juice. Bottled versions of liliko'i juice, syrup, curd and jelly are available in stores, but they are never as good as those prepared at home, so it's a good idea (and less expensive!) to make your own.

Liliko'i Juice

Makes 1 cup

Once you make the juice you're ready to go!

12 liliko'i

Making liliko'i juice is a somewhat messy process so it's a good idea to gather many fruit in order to make several cups at a time. Because recipes rarely require more than one cup of juice, freeze it in one cup plastic containers. For the smaller amounts used in cocktails, ice cube trays freeze a handy amount.

Wash fruit in sink or bucket to remove dirt, leaves and stems.

Cut all fruit in half and store in large bowl. Place sieve over medium bowl. Scoop pulp from liliko'i halves into sieve until 16 halves have been emptied. Save some seeds for garnish

purposes. Mash the rest of the pulp through sieve with wooden spoon until dry, seedy pulp is all that remains (discard pulp into compost bucket).

Pour juice into containers for refrigerator and freezer. Will keep at least 6 months.

Liliko'i Syrup

Makes 6 cups

Excellent in iced drinks and over frozen desserts!

4 cups water
6 cups sugar
2 cups liliko'i juice
1 teaspoon lemon juice (optional)
1/3 cup orange juice (optional)

Add sugar to water and heat to boiling point. Add juices to syrup and pour into plastic containers. Freeze in one cup containers.

Liliko'i Curd

Makes 4 cups

Use this as a topping for cakes, pies and morning toast!

2 cups sugar
2/3 cup butter
1 tablespoon lemon juice
6 eggs + 2 egg yolks
1 cup liliko'i juice

Cook sugar, butter, zest, eggs and juice in top of double boiler until almost as thick as mayonnaise. Pour into hot, sterilized jars and seal at once. Label and date. Will keep 6 to 8 months.

Homemade liliko'i curd is always a welcome gift for friends and family; keep some in the refrigerator to spread on toast for a perfect late afternoon snack.

Liliko'i Jelly

Makes 10 6 ounce jars

*Hot pepper liliko'i jelly is an unusual accompaniment
for meat, chicken and fish!*

3-1/2 cups liliko'i juice
7 cups sugar
6 Hawaiian chili peppers, sliced thin (optional)
2 tablespoons lemon zest (optional)
1 bottle liquid pectin

Combine juice, sugar, peppers and zest (if using). Bring to a
boil. Add the pectin immediately, stirring constantly. Bring
to a full rolling boil again for 30 seconds. Remove from heat.
Skim off any froth and
pour into sterilized
glasses and seal.
Label and date.
Will keep for 6
to 8 months.

Glossary

A

'Ahi
Hawaiian name for yellowfin or bigeye tuna. Also called shibi in Japanese. When the term 'ahi is used, it is assumed that fresh tuna, rather than canned, is meant.

C

Cointreau
An orange flavored liqueur; Grand Marnier or Triple Sec can be substituted.

Curd
A thick, cooked combination of citrus juice, sugar, eggs and butter used as a spread on toast or cakes.

K

Katakuriko
Japanese potato starch or flour.

Kinako
Japanese soy bean starch or flour.

L

Li Hing Mui
Chinese licorice and plum powder using as flavoring.

Liliko'i
The Hawaiian name for passion fruit which is grown in all tropical countries. In Spain, Central and South America and much of the Caribbean it is known as granadilla, but every country has its own name for the fruit: grenadille (France), maracuja (Portugal and Italy), magrandera (Zimbabwe), markisa (Indonesia), curuba (Cuba), lac tien (Vietnam), passhonfurutsu (Japan), Passionfrucht (Germany), etc.

Lillet
French apéritif wine; available in white (blanc) and red (rouge).

Limu
Hawaiian word for seaweed.

M

Macadamia Nuts
Rich, slightly sweet tree nuts that are a major crop in Hawai'i; often called 'Mac Nuts.' Walnuts or almonds can be substituted.

Mochi
Japanese candy treat made with rice flour.

Mochiko
Japanese rice flour.

N

Namasu
Japanese sweet pickle condiment, made quickly.

P

Passiflora Edulis
Latin name for the passion flower grown in Hawai'i that produces purple edible fruit.

Passiflora Edulis Flavicarpa
Latin name for the passion flower grown in Hawai'i that produces yellow edible fruit.

Passoa
Passion fruit liqueur made in France.

Poke
Hawaiian name for diced raw fish mixed with a few other ingredients (onion, seaweed, etc.).

Protein Powder
A vanilla flavored whey or soy powder that is added to smoothies for extra nutrition. Available in health food stores.

S

Salsa Verde
Mexican mixture of tomatillos, green chili peppers, onions and cilantro. Available in jars or cans.

Sriracha
Vietnamese hot chili pepper sauce, available in plastic squirt jars.

Sweet Chili Sauce
Thai hot sauce made of sugar, vinegar, garlic and hot peppers used as a dipping sauce or condiment.

Z

Zest
The colored portion of a citrus fruit rind, not including the bitter pith just below the colored portion.